Contents

Simple recipes for making everything from basic roast chicken to
easy pasta dishes for delicious midweek suppers.

Loaves and rolls that prove baking bread is not rocket science and
that fill any requirement from entertaining to sandwiches for work.

Become an outdoor grilling legend with recipes that demonstrate
there's more to cooking on a fire than turning a sausage or a chop
over and over.

A meaty chapter about what to do with everything from a whole
beef fillet to a duck breast with nice touches for entertaining.

Pizza is without a doubt the most important food-group for a bloke.
No matter what your favourite pizza joint offers, you can do better.

Big, hearty dishes for winter are the order of the day here, with
slow-cooked casseroles and a curry that will draw wild applause.

There just has to be pudding. Keep it simple but really, really
rich with the last chocolate dessert you will ever need to learn,
or a deadly crumble.

Sauces, side-dishes, starches and rice. These are all the little bits
and accompaniments to serve with everything that has gone before.

"When it comes to food, it's no longer cool for men to stare in confusion at pots and other kitchen stuff, meekly offering to wash dishes in exchange for meals. Social acceptance hinges on having a few killer recipes up your sleeve and a passing knowledge of what does what in the kitchen."

Introduction

This book is about getting blokes to cook. It's also about simple, honest cooking. With BLOKE in your pocket, you'll survive in any kitchen without too much trouble.

I have made my living in kitchens since I was sixteen years old, that's more than half my life. In that time, I've lost count of the number of times friends have proudly informed me that they have no idea how to cook but they are deadly with a take-away menu and a mobile phone.

Sadly, that's not going to score you any points with the fairer sex. Nor will it help you survive in a world where you are expected to take your share of the workload in the kitchen, be it in digs or a family home.

Experience has taught me that simplicity is the key to putting a good meal on the table, and food is only as good as the ingredients you use. I've also learned from years of designing menus and training relatively unskilled staff to run kitchens, that with some basic skills anyone can become a handy cook.

With this in mind, BLOKE has been structured to build things up slowly. We start out with a roast chicken that needs just five ingredients, including the chicken itself. From there it's just a short haul to cooking a Christmas turkey. We build up confidence with a simple fish supper and soon have you cooking a whole fish over hot coals or making a calamari stew.

Being a bloke is not an excuse for being useless in the kitchen. In fact, once you get into it, you will find that there is a lot about it to appeal to a bloke's sensibilities. There are lots of sharp knives, all kinds of gadgets, from special graters or pasta machines to fancy stoves and outdoor ovens. Best of all, you get to play with fire and be in charge at social gatherings.

BUILT FOR

COMFORT

Roast Chicken

1 whole free-range chicken
30ml olive oil
5 limes
salt and pepper

Preheat your oven to 200°C. Pat the bird's skin dry with paper towel or a tea towel. Place it in a roasting pan and rub the oil lightly into the skin, covering it all over. Halve 3 of the limes and squeeze the juice over the chicken, again rubbing it into all the nooks and folds.

Season with salt and pepper, and leave it with the legs and breasts uppermost. Cram 2 or 3 of the squeezed lime halves into the cavity and allow the chicken to stand for 30 minutes before you place it in the oven. Allowing it to 'rest' will give the seasoning time to develop and get the bird to room temperature.

When the oven is ready, place the roasting pan on a rack in the centre of the oven and cook for 45 minutes. Remove it from the oven and use a sharp knife to cut the skin connecting the leg to the breast. If you look into the cut and find the juices or meat to be pink still, make a similar cut on the other leg and return the chicken to the oven for 15 minutes. This time can vary depending on the size of the bird. Carve and serve with a wedge of lime, potatoes and peas, beans or broccoli.

If you like good old plain roast chicken, leave the limes out completely. This recipe is also fantastic for cooking outdoors on a kettle barbecue. Check after 45 minutes, and cook for a further 15 if required.

"Roast chicken is delicious and comforting. If you never learn another thing in the kitchen, at least master the roast chicken."

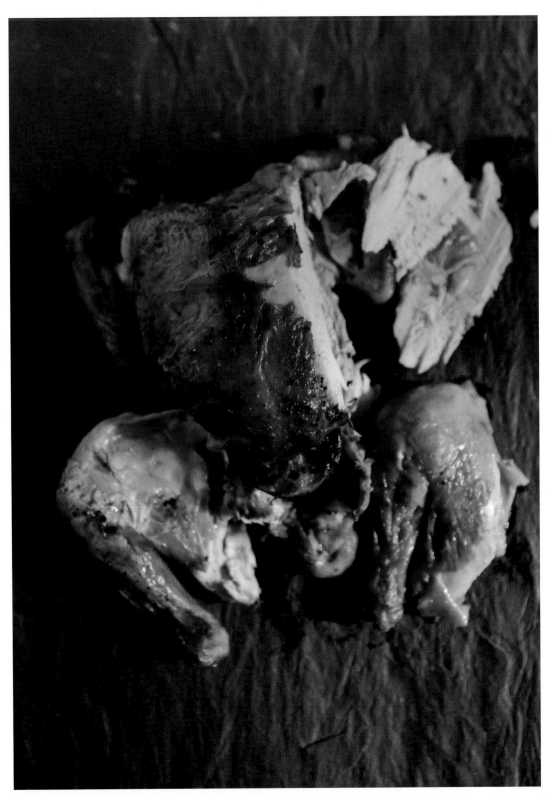

Fish & Chips

8 medium potatoes
30ml olive oil
30ml butter

800g frozen hake fillets
250ml flour for dusting
100ml butter
50ml olive oil
2 lemons
125ml white wine
10ml crushed garlic
30ml chopped parsley
30ml chopped dill
salt and pepper

Preheat your oven to 230°C. Wash the potatoes and cut them into rounds 2mm to 3mm thick. Place the olive oil and butter in a roasting pan and put it in the oven to heat. When the oil is sizzling, remove from the oven and scatter the potato rounds in the pan. Move them around with a wooden spoon to get oil on all of them. Return to the oven for 15 minutes, then turn it down to 200°C to cook for 30 to 45 minutes or until golden and crispy.

Make sure the fish is completely defrosted. You want fillets of consistent size and shape so they all cook at the same speed. Put the flour in a dish or bowl wide enough to hold the fish. Dredge each fillet in the flour to coat it lightly. Heat the butter and olive oil in a frying pan over a medium heat, and fry the fillets for 3 to 4 minutes on each side depending on their thickness. Season with salt and pepper as they cook.

When the last fillet is cooked, turn the heat up under the pan. Add the juice of the lemons and the wine to the cooking juices in the pan. Stir in the garlic and herbs and allow about half the liquid to boil away. Serve the fish with chips and green peas and the herb sauce.

"Fish makes a quick and easy mid-week meal, especially if you just want to have it with a salad."

Beef Burger

15ml olive oil
1 large onion
1kg ground beef
2 eggs
50ml chopped parsley
125ml soft breadcrumbs
salt and pepper

Heat the olive oil in a pan over a medium heat. Peel and finely chop the onion and gently fry it until it's soft but not coloured. Remove from the heat and cool to room temperature before combining with the meat.

Place the beef mince, fried onion, eggs, parsley and breadcrumbs in a mixing bowl. Use your hands to thoroughly combine the ingredients, adding salt and pepper to taste. Shape into 8 or 10 patties, depending on the size of your rolls. Don't make them too thin or they will dry out rapidly during cooking. They can be cooked on the stove in a pan, or on a flat grill over a fire.

Cook on one side over a medium heat until juice begins to appear on the top surface. Flip and cook for a further 3 to 4 minutes. You will quickly learn the cooking time for your preference of rare, medium or well done. However, to start with, cut into one of the patties after 3 or 4 minutes to check the centre. Serve on soft rolls with a selection of your favourite toppings and sauces.

Variation: By substituting lamb mince for beef and fresh, chopped oregano for parsley, you can make lamb burgers.

"Homemade burgers are ridiculously easy to make and great for entertaining big, hungry mobs."

Steak Roll

4 x 200g ostrich steaks
50ml olive oil
ground black pepper
crispy rolls
devilled mustard

This is a contemporary take on the standard steak roll, but you can do the same thing using beef fillet. Place the ostrich steaks in a dish or bowl where they can lie flat. Pour the olive oil over them and grind a generous amount of pepper over all. Turn the steaks over a few times to coat them well.

Cover the dish with clingfilm and leave it in the fridge for at least 3 hours or overnight. Before you intend to cook the steaks, get them out of the fridge and allow them to reach room temperature.

Steaks like this are best cooked in a grill pan, but a normal pan will do, or you can grill them over hot coals. Make sure the pan or grid is smoking hot so the steaks sizzle on contact.

Cook on one side until juices begin to ooze out of the top. Turn and cook on the other side for 3 minutes for medium or 5 for well done. Don't turn the meat over and over, as this will make it tough. Serve on rolls with devilled mustard or mushroom sauce. (See page 156.)

Variation: Add 5ml peri-peri sauce from the recipe on page 50 to the olive oil before coating the steaks.

"Marinating in olive oil is a handy trick to get steak or chicken breasts really tender."

Spag Bolognaise

500g lean beef mince
3 cloves garlic
1 onion
1 carrot
1 stick celery
30ml olive oil
60ml milk
400g tin chopped, peeled tomatoes
15ml tomato paste
250ml red wine
5ml sugar
salt and pepper
50ml chopped parsley
grated parmesan

Crush the garlic and finely chop the onion, carrot and celery, and gently fry them in the olive oil over a medium heat until they soften. Increase the heat and add the mince to cook for 2 to 3 minutes, stirring to break up any big lumps. Stir in the milk and allow it to evaporate completely before adding the chopped tomatoes and tomato paste. Allow to cook for 3 to 4 minutes before adding the wine and sugar, then season to taste.

Bring to the boil, then turn down to a very low simmer, so it's just bubbling gently, to cook for 1 to 1½ hours. Check it every 30 minutes or so, adding a little water if necessary. It should cook down to a dark, rich sauce.

Once it is ready, add the parsley and serve with a good quality spaghetti or penne and loads of parmesan. The instructions on pasta packaging are pretty foolproof. The recipe doubles perfectly if you need to feed more people or else freeze half the batch for later.

"Comfort food doesn't come any better than this highly adaptable staple for your repertoire."

Lasagne

90g butter
90g flour
1 litre milk
salt and pepper

1 portion bolognaise
1 box 'no-cook' lasagne sheets
grated mozzarella

Start by making a bechamel sauce. You need to melt the butter in a saucepan over a medium heat. Once it has melted, add the flour, stirring constantly until you have a smooth paste. Cook for 1 minute. Remove from the heat and pour the milk in slowly, whisking constantly to avoid lumps forming. When the milk is completely mixed in, return to the heat, still whisking as the sauce thickens. Bring it to the boil and remove from the heat.

To assemble your lasagne, start by smearing the base of a deep ovenproof dish with bechamel sauce. Cover this with sheets of lasagne, breaking them if necessary to fit your dish. You want a single layer here. If the sheets overlap, you end up with stodgy bits of pasta in the middle. Cover the pasta layer with about 1cm of bolognaise, then put more bechamel on this, more pasta sheets, and so on. You should have 3 or 4 layers with the last (top) covering being bechamel.

Sprinkle the top with grated cheese and bake at 200°C for 20 to 25 minutes. You can vary the topping to taste by using mozzarella, mature cheddar, parmesan or a combination. Serve with a crunchy green salad.

"Once you have mastered the art of making a good bolognaise, you can use it to make a legendary lasagne."

Pasta Basics

300g Italian '00' flour
3 eggs

Once you've weighed out the flour, tip it onto a work surface. Make a well in the centre of the flour and crack the eggs into it. Working quickly with a fork, draw in flour from the sides to mix with the eggs until it starts to come together into a ball.

As the ball forms, you want to use your hands to start kneading the dough. Cup your hand over the ball, and push it away from you, using the heel of your hand to flatten it as you go. Fold it in half and then in half again, and repeat the action. Do this for 2 minutes, then allow the dough to rest for 15 minutes. It should be dry and pliable.

Divide the dough into 12 even pieces, and form them into balls. Set the dial on the pasta machine to 1 and pass the first ball through the machine. Fold up the pasta and pass it through the machine again. Repeat until the same piece has been through on the first setting 5 times.

Now start changing the setting one click at a time, getting thinner and thinner as you go. You need to be continually dusting the pasta lightly with flour so it doesn't stick. Cut your strip of dough in half before rolling through the final and thinnest roller. Using whichever attachment you prefer, cut your pasta into spaghetti or linguine or leave it in sheets to use for lasagne.

Fresh pasta cooks very quickly. It needs only 2 minutes in boiling salted water. There are two quick and easy recipes overleaf to use with fresh pasta, but you can use it with any pasta sauce.

"In a kitchen, there are gadgets for everything, and a shiny pasta machine never disappoints."

Jason's Alfredo

400g cooked country ham
30ml butter
250ml cream
salt and pepper
500g tagliatelle

Cut the ham into strips and fry in the butter over a medium heat until crispy. Remove the ham from the pan leaving the juices behind. Add the cream and let it cook away for a few minutes until it has reduced in volume by half. Add the cooked pasta and the ham and toss through to make sure everything gets coated in the cream. Season and serve with a green salad.

Egg & Parmesan

500g spaghetti
100ml cooking liquid from pasta
1 egg
150g grated parmesan

Cook the pasta in boiling salted water, then drain, keeping 100ml of the cooking liquid. Return pasta to a large pan and keep the reserved liquid boiling in a saucepan alongside. Draw the pasta to one side of the pan and pour the beaten egg and pasta water into the gap. Place the pan over the heat and toss vigorously until the pasta is coated with egg. Add parmesan and toss until evenly distributed. Season and serve with a crunchy green salad.

Juicy Chicken Breasts

4 to 6 skinless chicken breast fillets

50ml olive oil
100ml lemon juice
sprig of rosemary
salt and pepper
OR
30ml sunflower oil
15ml sesame oil
100ml soy sauce
10ml crushed ginger
10ml crushed garlic
10ml honey

Place the chicken in a dish with a flat bottom. Mix the marinade ingredients in a cup. Pour this over the chicken, making sure it is well coated, then cover with clingfilm and place in the fridge for at least 3 hours.

Heat a pan over a high heat, then put the breasts in to cook and turn the heat down to medium. Cook for 5 minutes on the first side. Turn and cook for 4 minutes on the other side and turn once more to heat for 1 minute before slicing. Serve with a generous salad.

"These can be marinated in the morning, ready to cook in ten minutes when you get home."

DOUGH

NATION

Corn Bread

45ml sunflower oil
250ml milk
3 eggs
140g cake flour
165g maize meal
5ml salt
100g sugar
410g tin creamed sweetcorn

Fill a large pot (it needs to be big enough to hold a 2-litre steamer) a quarter way with water and bring to the boil. Lightly grease a fluted steamer and set aside. In a bowl, beat the oil, milk and eggs together. Place the flour, maize meal, salt and sugar in a separate bowl, and pour the sweetcorn on top.

Stir in the milk and egg mixture and combine well. Pour the batter into the prepared steamer and cover it with the lid. Carefully place the steamer in the pot with the boiling water and steam for 1½ hours. Check occasionally to see that the water hasn't all boiled away.

Remove the steamer from the pot and allow to cool for a while before turning it out onto a plate. It works with any grilled meat or chicken dish, especially at a barbeque. If there's anything left over, try toasting or even frying in a little butter with breakfast the next day.

"This is a reliable crowd-pleaser, and amazingly easy to make. Just measure, combine, stir and steam."

Brown Bread

600g brown bread or wholewheat flour
50g digestive bran
10g instant yeast
15ml salt
600ml lukewarm water
30ml sunflower oil
30ml honey
15ml sesame seeds
15ml poppy seeds
sunflower seeds to coat base and crust

Combine the flour, digestive bran, salt, sesame and poppy seeds. Sprinkle the little packet of yeast over the top of the mixture. Dissolve the honey and oil in the lukewarm water and pour this over the mixture. Mix to form a wet dough, adding a little more water if needed. The mixture should look like the top right image on the opposite page.

Grease a 26cm x 12cm loaf tin and coat the base with sunflower seeds. Transfer the dough from your mixing bowl and sprinkle liberally with more sunflower seeds. Put the loaf tin into a plastic shopping bag, tie it shut and let it sit for about 45 minutes, or until the dough has risen to the top of the tin. The time will vary according to the ambient temperature. In other words, it will take longer to rise in summer than in winter.

While the dough is rising, preheat your oven to 220°C. Remove the loaf tin from the shopping bag and place it on a rack in the centre of the oven. After 15 minutes turn the oven down to 180°C and bake for a further 45 minutes. Remove from the oven, turn the loaf out of the tin and put it back in the oven for a final 5 minutes to firm up the crust.

"Baking bread is incredibly satisfying, and producing a delicious loaf really isn't rocket science."

Fridge Rolls

500g white or wholewheat flour
30ml sugar
10ml salt
10g instant yeast
30ml melted butter
1 egg
375ml milk
white flour for dusting

Mix the flour, sugar, salt and yeast together in a bowl. Beat the egg into the milk and then stir this liquid into the dry ingredients, stirring with a wooden spoon until you have a smooth, even dough.

Cover the bowl with clingfilm and place in the fridge for at least 12 hours. It can be stored for up to 2 days in the fridge before you use it. When you are ready to bake, preheat your oven to 230°C. Shape into rolls and make 2 or 3 shallow slashes on each roll with a sharp knife.

Place on a lightly floured baking tray and dust the rolls lightly with a little white flour. Bake in the centre of the oven for 10 to 12 minutes, or until golden.

"This is one of the first bread recipes I ever learned and I still use it almost on a weekly basis."

Soda Bread

500g cake flour
5ml salt
5ml bicarbonate of soda
400ml buttermilk

Preheat your oven to 230°C. Sift the flour, salt and bicarb together into a bowl. Make a well in the centre and pour in the buttermilk, using one hand to mix in the flour from the sides of the bowl to form a ball. Turn out onto a floured surface and knead for a second to bring all the loose bits together into the ball. Place on a floured baking sheet and cut a cross in the top.

Place in the centre of the oven to bake for 15 minutes, then reduce the oven temperature to 200°C. Bake for a further 30 minutes until golden brown.

A good trick to check if a loaf of bread is done is to tap the bottom with your fingernail. If it sounds hollow, then it is baked through. Like all tricks, this one takes a bit of practice, so the more bread you bake, the better you will be at gauging baking time.

"This traditional Irish loaf requires no yeast or rising time. Mix, pop it in the oven and serve a fresh loaf."

Pot Bread

900g flour
15ml salt
10g instant yeast
625ml warm water
30ml melted butter
1 egg

You need a 30cm cast-iron pot with a lid and a charcoal or wood fire for this recipe. Mix the flour, salt and yeast in a bowl. Add the water and butter and mix to form a stiff dough. Turn it out onto a lightly floured kitchen surface and knead for 10 to 15 minutes until the dough is smooth and elastic.

Return the dough to a bowl and cover it with clingfilm. Find a warm spot in the kitchen and leave it there to rise until it doubles in size. Once it has doubled, knead again for 3 minutes, then cut into 8 equal pieces, rolling each into a ball. Place 7 balls around the edge of your greased cast-iron pot, placing the 8th in the middle.

Beat the egg in a cup, using a fork, and brush this egg wash over the rolls. Cover with the lid and allow to rise for 20 minutes. When you are ready to bake, remove the pot lid, place a single sheet of newspaper over the pot and replace the lid. This will help create a good seal. If you want, you can trim the paper, but it will burn off anyway.

Set the pot on a bed of hot coals and place a spadeful of coals on the lid. Bake for 45 to 60 minutes. Allow to cool completely before turning the bread out of the pot and breaking it into rolls.

"Baking bread on a fire is a neat trick and a really strong addition to a bloke's credentials."

MISSION

Pork Ribs

3.5kg fresh pork ribs
50ml honey

Marinade
150ml tomato sauce
150ml light soy sauce
40ml hoisin sauce
50ml olive oil
50ml rice wine vinegar
50ml grated ginger
50ml crushed garlic
45ml brown sugar

Start a day ahead, as you need time for the flavours in the marinade to develop. Note that they are pre-cooked in the oven before grilling to ensure proper cooking and tenderness.

Place the ribs in a large, non-metallic bowl. Mix all the marinade ingredients together in a separate bowl and pour over the ribs, making sure they are well coated. Cover and marinate overnight in the refrigerator, turning them at least once during the process.

Preheat your oven to 180°C. Divide the ribs between two large roasting pans and cover with tin foil. Roast for 45 to 60 minutes until soft and tender. Once this is done, you need to finish them over coals or under the grill. We prefer coals for a smoky flavour.

Use about 50ml of the leftover juice in the pans to mix with the honey. Baste the ribs with this before cooking. Place the ribs on a grid over hot coals, turning them once they start to catch and get a bit of burn on them. They are ready when the other side is cooked to a similar degree.

"You could probably open a rib joint with this recipe – it truly is a bone-sucking sauce."

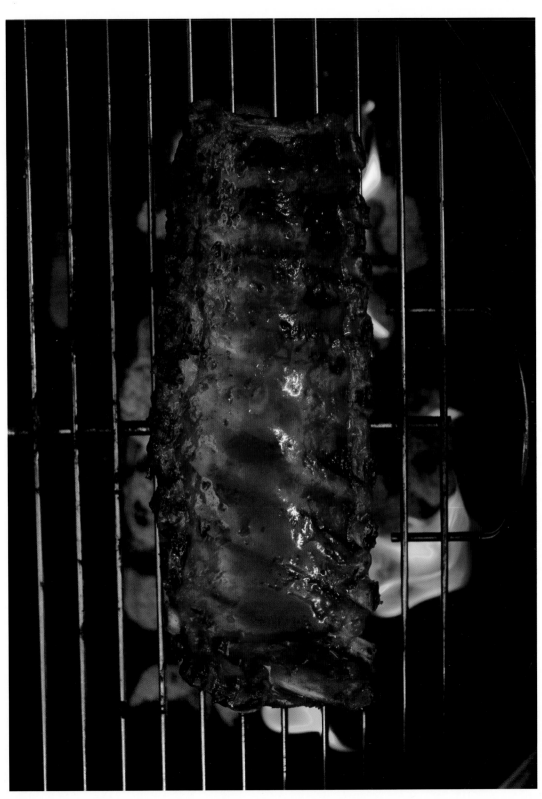

Sosaties

1kg cubed lamb
8 skewer sticks
2 onions
15ml sunflower oil
15ml curry powder
15ml apricot jam
15ml dried oregano
5ml ground cumin
5ml ground ginger
125ml white wine vinegar
salt and pepper
1 red pepper
1 yellow pepper
16 bay leaves

You need to start making this a day ahead. Halve and slice the onions, and gently fry them in the oil until they soften but don't colour. Stir in the curry powder, jam, oregano, cumin and ginger and cook for 2 minutes. Tip in the vinegar and allow this to bubble away for 3 or 4 minutes, then remove from the heat and cool.

When it is cool enough, purée the spice and onion mixture in a food processor or with a stick blender. Place the mixture in a bowl and toss in the lamb, stirring to make sure it is well coated, then cover with clingfilm and marinate overnight in the fridge.

An hour before you make the skewers, soak the sticks in water to stop them burning too badly over the coals. Seed the peppers, cut the flesh into chunks, and tear the bay leaves in half.

Thread the marinated meat onto the sticks, starting with lamb, then bay leaf, a piece of pepper and another cube of lamb. You should end up with 5 pieces of lamb per skewer. Grill over hot coals for 3 to 4 minutes each on two sides.

"This is a messy affair, but the effort is worth it."

Boerewors

500g minced fatty pork
1.5kg minced beef
10ml whole allspice
15ml coriander seeds
5ml freshly ground black pepper
30ml biltong spice
dehydrated sausage casings

Ask your butcher for a bit of input to get you going on this. Ask him to sell you a small amount of biltong or boerewors spice and some sausage casings. This recipe will make 2kg of boerewors, but it is easily doubled.

Place the allspice (also called pimento) and coriander seeds in a dry pan and roast over a medium heat until they start to brown. Move to a spice grinder or a mortar and pestle and grind finely. Mix with the boerewors spice and black pepper. Place all the meat in a mixing bowl and scatter half the spices on top. Use your hands to mix the meat together as well as possible, then scatter the rest of the spice over it and mix again.

Soak the sausage casings in water for 30 minutes before you use them. A sausage machine is good for the next bit, but you can make do with a stainless steel or even a plastic funnel. Pull the casing up over the spout of the funnel and tie a knot in the end. Feed the sausage filling into the funnel and push it through into the casing. As the casing fills up, it will come off the spout. Use one hand to stop it coming away too quickly.

When you have filled the casing, you can coil it into one large rustic roll or twist it off into individual sausages. Cook over medium coals and serve with potato salad, lime mayo corn (see overleaf) and a green salad.

"You can manage this with a few simple implements, there's no need to go buying a sausage machine to start with."

Buffalo Wings

2 dozen chicken wings
100ml soy sauce
100ml tomato sauce
100ml hoisin sauce
30ml rice wine vinegar
10ml grated ginger
5ml sugar
salt and pepper

Combine all the ingredients in a bowl and mix well, ensuring that the sugar dissolves completely. If you want to make it ahead or cover less wings, the sauce will keep in a sealed jar in the fridge for up to 3 weeks.

Marinate the wings in the sauce for 2 to 3 hours and then grill them over medium coals for 15 minutes, turning constantly to avoid excessive charring.

Lime Mayo Corn

6 ears sweetcorn
4 limes
100g soft butter
50ml mayonaisse
salt and pepper

This very simple recipe will elevate the simple pleasure of grilled corn to a legendary event. Combine the juice of the limes in a bowl with the butter and mayonnaise. Season with salt and pepper, and baste the corn liberally with this mixture as they cook over the coals. Serve straight from the fire.

Peri-peri Flattie

20 chillies
5 cloves garlic
50ml white wine vinegar
125ml olive oil

1 large chicken
2 lemons

This recipe makes far more peri-peri sauce than you will need for one bird, but it keeps in a sealed bottle in the fridge for up to 4 weeks. Once you have the recipe, you can adjust the chilli heat or garlic content to taste.

Roughly chop the chillies with the seeds, and place them in a blender with the peeled garlic. With the motor running, add the vinegar through the opening in the lid of the blender. Once this is in, pour the oil in a slow, steady stream until the mixture takes on a creamy look – about 3 to 4 minutes. Switch off and bottle the sauce until needed.

Have your butcher spatchcock the chicken, or do it yourself with a heavy cook's knife or some poultry shears. Cut through the breastbone (not the spine) of the chicken. Open it out and lay it on a board, then bash the spine with the heel of your hand so the chicken stays flat. Transfer to a dish and brush all over with peri-peri sauce and leave for 2 to 3 hours before cooking.

Grill over a good bed of medium coals, skin side up for 20 minutes. Turn and cook on the skin side for 10 to 15 minutes, then turn and heat through for 5 minutes. A flattie does well in a kettle barbecue over indirect coals and can also be cooked, skin side up, in a conventional oven at 220°C for 45 minutes.

"This peri-peri sauce is so versatile, chicken is just the beginning. It goes on anything, from steak to prawns."

Rib-eye

4 x 250g steaks
50ml olive oil
pepper

Cooking a steak starts with choosing the right cut of meat. Fillet's ok,
but there are better uses for it than cutting it into steaks. You want the
tastier cuts like sirloin, rump and the delicious rib-eye for the fire. As you
try different cuts, ask your butcher to vary the thickness of the meat, from
say 3cm to 5cm, to find the steak that works for you.

Place the steaks in a flat dish and pour the olive oil over them. Grind black
pepper over them to taste and then flip them over in the oil to coat them
properly. You can cover them if necessary, but don't put them in the fridge;
you want them at room temperature when you cook them.

Steaks should be cooked over very hot coals. They should sizzle as they hit
the grid. Cook on one side until you see blood start to come through on the
top (raw) side. Turn the steaks and cook them for a further 3 to 5 minutes
depending on whether you prefer rare or medium.

"The trick here is in the timing.
You won't get it right first time, but
with practice you can become a
stellar griller."

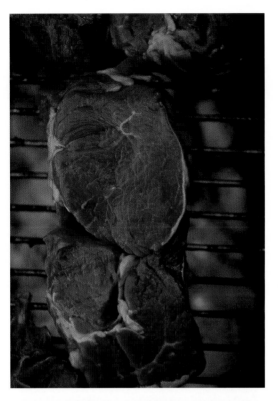

Whole Fish

1 fish
50ml soft butter
15ml chopped parsley
1 lemon
15ml olive oil

You want a whole fish with firm white flesh. Unless you catch it yourself and are used to cleaning and scaling the ocean's bounty, get the fishmonger to do it. It's best to cook it on the day you buy it, but if you need to refrigerate it, only do so overnight.

Spread the butter all over the inside of the fish and sprinkle the parsley evenly throughout. Lay thin slices of lemon inside; about half the lemon will do. Keep the other half to squeeze over the fish while it cooks. Close the fish and cut two or three slashes in the skin on each side, then rub the skin all over with the olive oil.

You will notice that the recipe only requires small amounts of inputs like parsley and olive oil. This is because white fish has a delicate flavour and you don't want to overpower it with strong herbs or other ingredients. You can vary amounts to taste.

Place it in a folding grid like the one in the picture as this will make it simple to turn the fish while it cooks. You need medium coals for this as the fish cooks quickly and will burn and dry out if the fire is too hot. When the skin is crisping and pulling away from the slashes in the sides, it is done. Serve with boiled potatoes or a potato salad and a nice, chunky Greek salad.

"The folding grid really is essential for cooking fish on the fire; it makes turning the fish during cooking much easier."

Crayfish

12 crayfish tails
75ml butter
50ml olive oil
30ml vermouth
5ml crushed garlic
15ml chopped dill
30ml chopped parsley

Cleaning crayfish is a bit of a mission. It's messy and repetitive, but the reward is a feast of stunningly sweet, rich flesh. Take scissors and snip the top of the shell along its length, following the intestine. This allows you to remove the offending line before you cut through the flesh with a sharp knife to butterfly the crustacean.

Over a medium heat, melt the butter in a saucpan and stir in the olive oil until it combines. Pour in the vermouth, add the garlic and herbs, give it a quick stir and remove from the heat. Use this mixture as a baste for the crayfish as you cook them and reserve some to pour over at the end.

Crayfish, like prawns and other shellfish, take just minutes to cook. About 3 minutes on one side and 2 on the other is all they need. As soon as the flesh loses its jelly-like apearance and goes opaque, they are done. You will also notice the shell colour becoming vibrant almost as soon as they hit the heat.

"Don't wander off while these are on the fire or they will be ruined. The delicate flesh cooks very quickly."

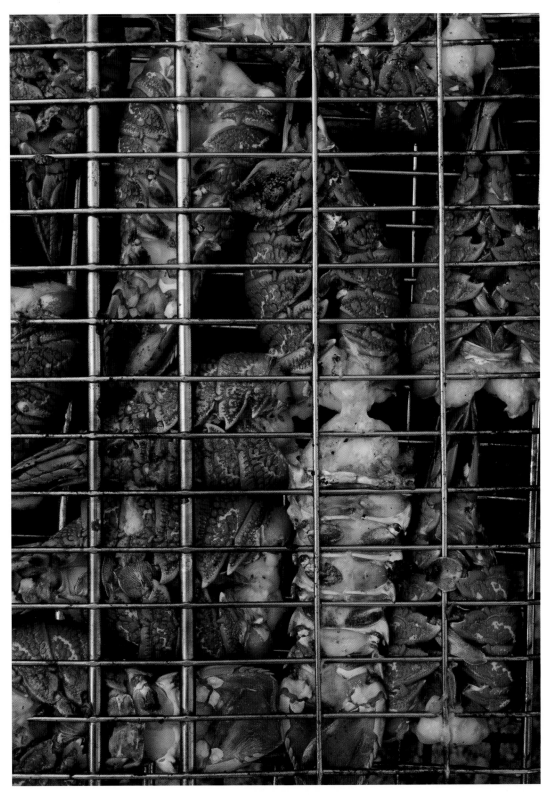

Festive Turkey

1 medium turkey
½ loaf sliced white bread
2 onions
200g butter
1 bunch sage
1 bunch flatleaf parsley
250ml cream

500ml dry white wine
hickory chips for the fire

Cooking a festive turkey is as much about the stuffing as anything else, so that's the starting point. You need to buy the bread a couple of days ahead so that it is stale, then whiz it in a blender, with the crust on, to make crumbs.

Finely chop the onions and gently fry them in the butter until soft. Remove from the heat and chop the sage and parsley very finely, then add them to the onions along with the bread and cream. Stir all this together to combine well.

When the stuffing is completely cool, loosen the skin on top of the bird and push a good handful in there. Move it around to form an even layer which will keep the breast-meat moist. Use the rest of the stuffing to fill the cavity of the bird and pop it in the fridge while you get the fire ready.

You need to build an indirect fire in your kettle grill, ensuring you have plenty of coals. Place a foil drip pan in the centre and pour in the wine. This will keep the bird moist as it cooks and catch any juices dripping from it. Scatter the hickory chips on the coals; this will give the skin a distinctive reddish hue.

Place the bird in the centre of the grid and close with the lid. It should take up to 2 hours to cook like this. You can check if it's ready by cutting between the leg and breast like a roast chicken.

"If you take charge of the turkey from the outset, the trimmings and veggies become someone else's problem."

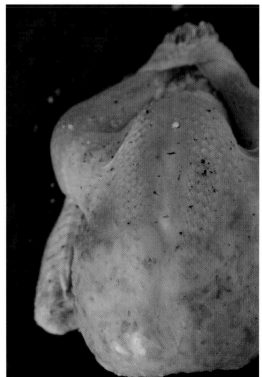

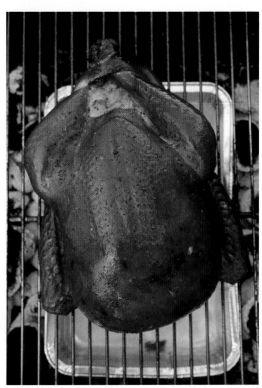

Toasties

sliced white bread
sliced ham or other cold cuts
edam or mature cheddar cheese
tomatoes
onions
butter

The toasted sandwich is the forgotten hero of feeding schemes for blokes. You need a fire, a folding grid, bread and some fillings. The classic is ham, cheese, tomato and onion, but filling options are limited only by budget or imagination.

Lay slices of bread on one half of the folding grid. Pile the fillings on these slices. Place another slice of bread on top of each one and close and secure the grid. Melt some butter in a saucepan until it is completely liquid and then take the butter and the grid out to the fire. A good bed of medium coals is best for this.

Brush one side of the sandwiches with melted butter and place the folding grid, buttered side down, on the grid of your charcoal grill. Brush the top of the sandwiches with more butter and cook until golden underneath before flipping and toasting the other side.

Break out the beers and keep making toasties in relays until fillings or appetites give in.

"I once lived on toasties for an entire fishing trip. We kept making runs for beer, bread and cheese."

Potjie

1kg cubed chuck steak
30ml flour
salt and pepper
50ml sunflower oil
1 large onion
750ml beef stock
250ml sherry
6 potatoes
500g cubed butternut
1 punnet green beans
2 punnets patty pans
1 punnet baby corn

Build a fire and make sure you have a surface like a table near the fire where
you can place or chop ingredients. Place the flour in a bowl and season it with
salt and pepper. Toss the meat in the flour to coat it lightly and set it aside.

Chop the onion quite roughly and place your cast-iron pot on the fire. Don't
thrust it into the heart of the blaze, but find a place on the fire where the heat is
mild and you can place coals around the base to control temperature.

Heat the oil and brown the meat in batches until it is well coloured. Transfer
the sealed meat to a bowl. Now cook the onions in the juices from the meat.
When they have softened, pour in the sherry and, with a wooden spoon,
scrape all the bits that have stuck to the pot. Pour in the beef stock and stir
in the meat, cover and simmer for up to 2 hours over a gentle heat.

Peel and quarter the potatoes and add them to the potjie to cook for 5 minutes
before adding the butternut. Once these are tender, you can add the green beans,
halved patty pans and the baby corn to cook on top of the other ingredients for
10 to 15 minutes. Only stir them in when you are ready to serve with rice.

"Cooking in a cast-iron pot
on an open fire is kind of a rite
of passage for a bloke."

Firestarter

Some attention should be given to the matter of making a fire. As a bloke, you are expected to know how to make a fire. It's an assumption that follows you around until your mother-in-law tosses you a box of matches and asks you to sort the fire out for the family get-together. It should be a basic skill, but a lot of guys haven't got the first clue.

You have four choices when it comes to cooking over a fire. You can use charcoal, briquettes, wood or gas. I think gas is a bit of a non-starter because the point of cooking on a fire is to get the smoky flavour.

Briquettes are fine for a kettle braai, although for grilling meat, they tend to give off a chemical flavour at peak heat and are much better for indirect cooking when you actually want them cooling as they heat the space under the lid.

Charcoal is convenient and gives you a bed of usable coals very quickly. Quality is always an issue though, so you need to find a brand you trust and try to stick with it. I can't count the times I've bought a bag of charcoal on a fishing trip and found it to consist of a few black lumps and a lot of dust.

As a rule, I tend to choose a wood fire to cook on as it imparts the best flavour and allows you to build a big bed of coals. Wherever possible I try to use wood cut by people removing alien species from river systems, or collect the pruning matter from grape vines or olive trees.

The classic Boy Scout method, of placing two split logs as a base then two on top at right angles and then building until you have a sort of pyramid, works like a bomb. You put some smaller twigs and paper or a firelighter in the centre and it goes in seconds.

Once the flames have died down, you want to keep checking the coals by holding your hand over them. For steak, you should only be able to hold your hand 5cm above the grid for a count of 3 before it's too hot to handle. For chicken and fish, the count for medium coals is 8.

"Playing with fire is half the fun of cooking outdoors."

FLESHY

PARTS

Whole Fillet

1.2kg beef fillet
100ml olive oil
black pepper
1 sprig rosemary
15ml wholegrain mustard
15ml Dijon mustard

Marinate in olive oil and pepper (no salt or it'll dry out) overnight. Preheat the oven to 230°C. Tie the thinner end of the fillet onto the main body so that the entire fillet is the same thickness throughout and will cook evenly. Slip a sprig of rosemary under the twine.

Mix the wholegrain and Dijon mustards together and rub this over the whole fillet. Place in a baking tray and cook in the oven for the following times:
15 to 20 minutes for rare
20 to 25 minutes for medium-rare
25 to 30 minutes for medium

You can also do the fillet in a kettle grill over an indirect fire with the lid on. Use the above times as a guide. Serve with caramelised onions, griddled leeks and new potatoes. It's even better with the devilled mustard from page 156 drizzled over it.

"Cooking a perfect fillet is no biggie, it just requires a bit of practice. It's an easy, no-fuss meal for entertaining."

Lamb Chops

6 lamb chops

Rub
15ml dried oreganum
15ml whole coriander
15ml paprika
15ml sugar
5ml black peppercorns
5ml dried chilli

Place all the rub ingredients in a pestle and bash and grind with a mortar to make a fine powder. Rub this onto the lamb chops, and leave them covered for an hour or two before cooking.

For best results, cook them in a smoking-hot grill pan brushed with a little olive oil. You can do these on a fire too, they take about 3 minutes on each side, unless you like yours well done. Lamb chops are great with mash and peas or you can brave couscous by following the instructions on the packet.

"This is a good moment to go out and invest in a grill pan. They make a huge difference to the flavour of any meat you cook in them."

Apple Pork Chops

6 pork chops
black pepper
4 golden delicious apples
50ml butter
30ml sugar
50ml good whisky

Cut nicks into the fat of the chops so they don't curl up when you cook them. Season with black pepper and preheat your oven to 200°C. Core the apples and then cut them into manageable segments. Heat a pan and cook the pork chops for 2 minutes on each side to brown them. Transfer to a roasting dish and place them in the oven for 10 to 15 minutes.

Melt the butter in the same pan you used to cook the chops. Add the sugar and allow it to melt before adding the apples. Toss the apples and cook them until they start to go brown and sticky. Pour in the whisky and allow it to hiss and evaporate. Remove the chops from the oven and serve with the caramelised apples and either mash or potato salad with broccoli for greens.

"This is another one of my quick dinner fixes, especially something for entertaining a couple of mates midweek."

Pork Shoulder

1.5kg shoulder of pork (bone in)
50ml fennel seeds
2ml dried chilli
5ml flaked salt
2ml ground pepper

Preheat your oven to 230°C. Using a very sharp kitchen knife, score the skin of the pork lengthways and across. Transfer to a baking tray and place on a rack in the centre of the oven for 20 minutes until the fat is getting crispy. Remove from the oven and turn the heat down to 150°C.

Mix the chilli, fennel, salt and pepper and pound in a pestle and mortar. Rub this over the skin of the pork, working it into the cuts you have made. Return it to the oven to cook for 2½ to 3 hours.

"I'm fussy about the origins of any pork I use because I used to raise my own pigs. Pigs farmed on a small scale are always a good bet."

Ostrich Steak

4 x 200g ostrich steaks
50ml olive oil
5ml ground pepper

Bearnaise Sauce
1 lemon
250g butter
3 egg yolks

Ostrich is a lovely lean meat which is the perfect foil for the rich indulgence of bearnaise. Place the steaks in a flat dish and marinate in the oil and pepper overnight or for at least 3 hours before cooking. Preheat your oven to 230°C.

To make the bearnaise, you need a hand blender. Making it with a whisk will probably finish you for the rest of the day. Juice the lemon, then place the butter in a saucepan over a medium heat to melt and begin to bubble.

Use the blender to blend the egg yolks and lemon juice in a mixing bowl. As you blend, pour the hot butter into the egg mixture in a steady stream. Continue until the butter is finished and the mixture is well combined. It should be pale yellow and silky smooth, like a thick mayonnaise.

Cook the steaks to taste on a smoking-hot grill pan. Serve with potatoes, wilted greens and bearnaise sauce on the side.

"The meat is kind of incidental in this recipe. You can cook a beef steak using this method. The real prize is the bearnaise."

Quail

6 quail
30ml butter
30ml honey

The trick here is to get your hands on quail. It's something you very seldom see in a supermarket, but an old-fashioned butcher should have a contact or two. The alternative is to hunt them yourself, but that's a story on its own.

Preheat the oven to 200°C. Wash the birds under a running tap and pat them dry. Cut them in half through the breastbone and then along the spine. Season with salt and pepper. Melt butter and honey together in a saucepan and keep it handy.

Heat a grill pan until smoking hot and place the quail skin-side down for 3 minutes, then turn them and cook for a further 3 minutes. Remove from the stove top and brush the skin side liberally with the butter mixture. Now place the pan with the quail in the oven for 10 minutes.

You can also cook quail by putting them in the oven at 200°C for 10 minutes. Remove and baste them, then return them to the oven for 10 more minutes. Serve with oven chips and a Greek salad.

"Growing up in a family of bird hunters has given me access to all kinds of game birds, but quail is my hands-down favourite."

Duck & Noodles

4 duck breasts
4 x 100g portions of egg noodles
5ml sesame oil
15ml soy sauce
15ml rice wine vinegar
5ml sugar
1 small red chilli, seeded and chopped
2ml wasabi powder
salt and pepper
2 heads bok choy
4 spring onions
1 cucumber

You need a pan that can go in the oven for this, and you should preheat the oven to 200°C. Diagonally score the skin, season with salt and pepper and place skin side down in a hot pan for 3 minutes. Turn and cook for a further 3 minutes. Remove from heat and place in the oven for 5 minutes. It should still be pink inside but not bloody. Remove from the oven and rest.

Meanwhile, make a dressing by mixing the sesame oil, soy sauce, rice wine vinegar, sugar, chilli, salt, pepper and wasabi in a cup. Place the noodles in gently boiling water until they soften. Drain, and toss with the bok choy leaves and sliced spring onion. Pour the dressing over this and arrange in 4 bowls.

Slice the duck breast into 2cm pieces and serve on the noodles with a garnish of cucumber ribbons made by shaving the cucumber with a potato peeler.

"This is a very quick but impressive dinner. Definitely one for the ladies."

TO BASE

Pizza Companion

Although it helps, you don't really need a wood-fired oven to make excellent pizza. There are a couple of rules and tools, but you can make the best pizza you'll ever eat right in your kitchen or on a kettle grill in the back yard.

The first thing you need is a terracotta tile. The thing about cooking pizza is that you need to dry out the base as you cook it. If you put it on a metal baking tray, it sweats and gets soggy. In a pizza oven, the base is in contact with clay bricks which wick away the moisture in the dough.

An unglazed terracotta tile from a building supplier works like the brick floor of a pizza oven, absorbing and dispersing moisture during cooking. You'll see adverts for fancy pizza stones, but a few bucks will get you a perfectly serviceable tile. You may have to cut it to fit your oven, but then you are a bloke after all.

The next trick is to understand the importance of heat. Pizza needs lots of it. You need to turn a domestic oven up as high as possible without putting the grill element on. Alternatively, a nice, big bed of coals in a kettle grill will do the trick. Place the tile on the centre rack of the oven or on the grill of the kettle to get hot before you put the pizza on it.

Ideally you should have a paddle to move the pizza from preparation surface to baking surface. However, with a good pair of heat-proof gloves you can just remove the hot tile from the oven, slap the base on it and do the toppings before returning the pizza to cook.

One of those cicular pizza cutters is a real asset to your gadget collection here, and the paddle is a definite boon, especially if you ever go the whole hog and build an oven. If you are cooking in a kettle grill, it is also worth getting a relatively cheap, free-standing oven thermometer to help you monitor the temperature under the lid.

"Pizza is the perfect bloke meal. You eat it with your hands, and all the food groups are gathered into one serving."

Pizza Dough

700g cake flour
5ml salt
10g instant yeast
375ml lukewarm water
30ml olive oil

This is a basic, all-purpose pizza dough for your bases. It is very simple to make and does not require much skill. As your pizza skills and tastes improve, you may want to scout around for other recipes. Everyone who makes pizza seems to have a special variation.

Measure the flour and salt into a mixing bowl and sprinkle the dry yeast over the surface. Measure the lukewarm water in a measuring jug and add the olive oil to it. Pour the liquid over the dry ingredients and leave it to bubble for 2 minutes just to let the warm water activate the yeast.

Use a wooden spoon to start mixing the flour and water, stirring until it comes together and is too thick to stir. Remove the dough as a single lump from the bowl and start to knead it on a lightly floured surface. The technique is the same as for making pasta. Place the folded-up dough under the palms of your hands, and push away from yourself, using the heels of your hands to flatten the dough as you go. It must be kneaded for 15 minutes until the dough is smooth and elastic and does not break when stretched.

Form into a ball, place in a clean, lightly floured bowl and cover with clingfilm. Leave in a warm part of the kitchen to rise until the dough doubles in size. Depending on the weather, this could take 30 minutes or up to 2 hours.

Variation: You can make a wholewheat pizza base by changing flour content. Instead of 700g cake flour, use 350g cake flour and 350g wholewheat. Then use 400ml lukewarm water, not 375ml. Follow the same process to make the dough, but bear in mind that it will rise slower than the white dough.

"You could probably use frozen bases, but then why bother making your own pizza in the first place?"

Neapolitan Sauce

2 medium onions
30ml olive oil
10ml crushed garlic
2 x 410g tins chopped tomatoes
5ml sugar
salt and pepper
10 fresh basil leaves

Finely chop the onions and gently fry them in the olive oil in a pot with a
thick base. When they have softened but not coloured, add the garlic and
cook for a further minute or so. Add the tomatoes and sugar, and season
with salt and pepper. Bring to the boil, then reduce the heat and simmer
slowly for 30 to 45 minutes, or until the liquid is reduced by one third.

Tear up the basil leaves and add them about 2 minutes before you finish
cooking the sauce. You can use it on pizza bases as it is or purée it
for a smoother texture.

The sauce will keep in the fridge for a week or it freezes very well. It is
the very heart of a good pizza, but can also be used for pasta sauces or
be served with grilled steak.

"It's a simple thing, but
your tomato sauce can make
or break a pizza."

Toppings

When it comes to toppings, it's hardly worth putting down recipes as personal tastes vary so wildly. Everyone has his favourites, which makes for an interesting collection of ingredients at a bring-and-share pizza party.

I've got some suggestions for pizzas I really enjoy. Use them if you like, or gather some ideas and make up your own. The last 4 toppings require that you partially cook the base with a little Neapolitan sauce on it, before adding the ingredients.

Salami, anchovies and green olives.

Smoked chicken, peppadews and feta.

Green and red peppers, black forest ham, mushrooms, black olives.

Griddled aubergine and zucchini, roast red and yellow peppers, parmesan.

Caramelised onions, camembert, pine kernels and fresh oregano.

Salmon, cream cheese and avocado.

Sliced fresh tomato, baby mozzarella balls and basil leaves.

Parma ham, rocket and shaved parmesan.

"If you make up raw pizzas on lightly floured wax paper, they are easy to slide onto a baking stone or pizza paddle."

Calzone

1 pizza base
salami
mozzarella
onions

Cover the entire pizza base with Neapolitan sauce (see page 90), leaving a
1cm rim right around the edge. Build up your toppings on one half only,
being quite liberal with the ones you like best. You can use any fillings you
like if you think they will go together.

Remember that the flavours are going to mingle far more in this cooking
method than on a pizza, as it cooks longer. I tend to avoid too many
anchovies or olives, but that's just me. I like a simple thing like salami,
mozzarella and a little onion in a calzone.

Fold the unadorned half of the pizza base over to cover the other half and
press the edges together with a fork. Transfer to a pizza paddle and place
on the cooking surface. Allow the crust to crisp and start to go golden
before removing it.

"I always make calzone at the end
of a session with the pizza oven.
They are excellent cold or warmed
up for lunch the next day.
Of course, you might like them
straight off the paddle."

Toys for Boys

There are loads of gadgets to play with when you start getting serious about cooking. You just have to wander through a kitchen store or look at outdoor grills, cookers and barbecues to realise how huge the array of toys for cooking boys actually is. My favourite culinary toy of all time has to be my wood-fired oven.

We built a pizza oven on our farm some years back and it became a focal point of our social life. More recently, my sister built one in her back yard in Cape Town. Geting it lit and building up the temperature is a ritual in itself. Then, having everyone sitting around as you cook everything from a starter of prawns to pizzas and even bread is a great way to pass a lazy day.

These ovens have become massively popular in the US and Australia in recent years, and if you enjoy an outdoor lifestyle, it's easy to understand why. This one was built by brothers Charl and Rudi de Lange who have a small artisanal business crafting bespoke pizza and bread ovens.

Building one requires a bit of space and the boys from Fire Oven took about two weeks from start to finish. Once it's done it needs to be cured with a series of fires growing larger with each burn. Your eventual aim is to get the peak temperature in the oven to around 350°C before backing it off to around 300°C for pizza. The only way to learn, as Rudi says, is to make fire.

As the oven cools, and it does this really slowly due to its heat-retaining properties, you can use it to cook all kinds of stuff. On a weekend, we will typically light a fire and roast some peppers and aubergines to have as starters with some focaccia bread. Next we'll start doing rounds of pizzas with different toppings for lunch.

Once the pizza is done, the coals come out and bread goes in. Bread is followed by a slow casserole in a cast-iron pot which will serve us for Sunday lunch. Baking in these ovens relies on the slow release of the heat retained in the special fire-bricks that make up the inner chamber. If you close the door, it takes something like 15 to 20 hours for the oven to cool completely. There's plenty you can do with that heat.

Ovens of this approximate design have been in use for millennia, and it's incredibly satisfying getting one to work for you. It's also a lot of fun to have a bunch of mates over and be the one in charge of the paddle.

"Playing with fire is half the fun of cooking outdoors."

SLOW

BURN

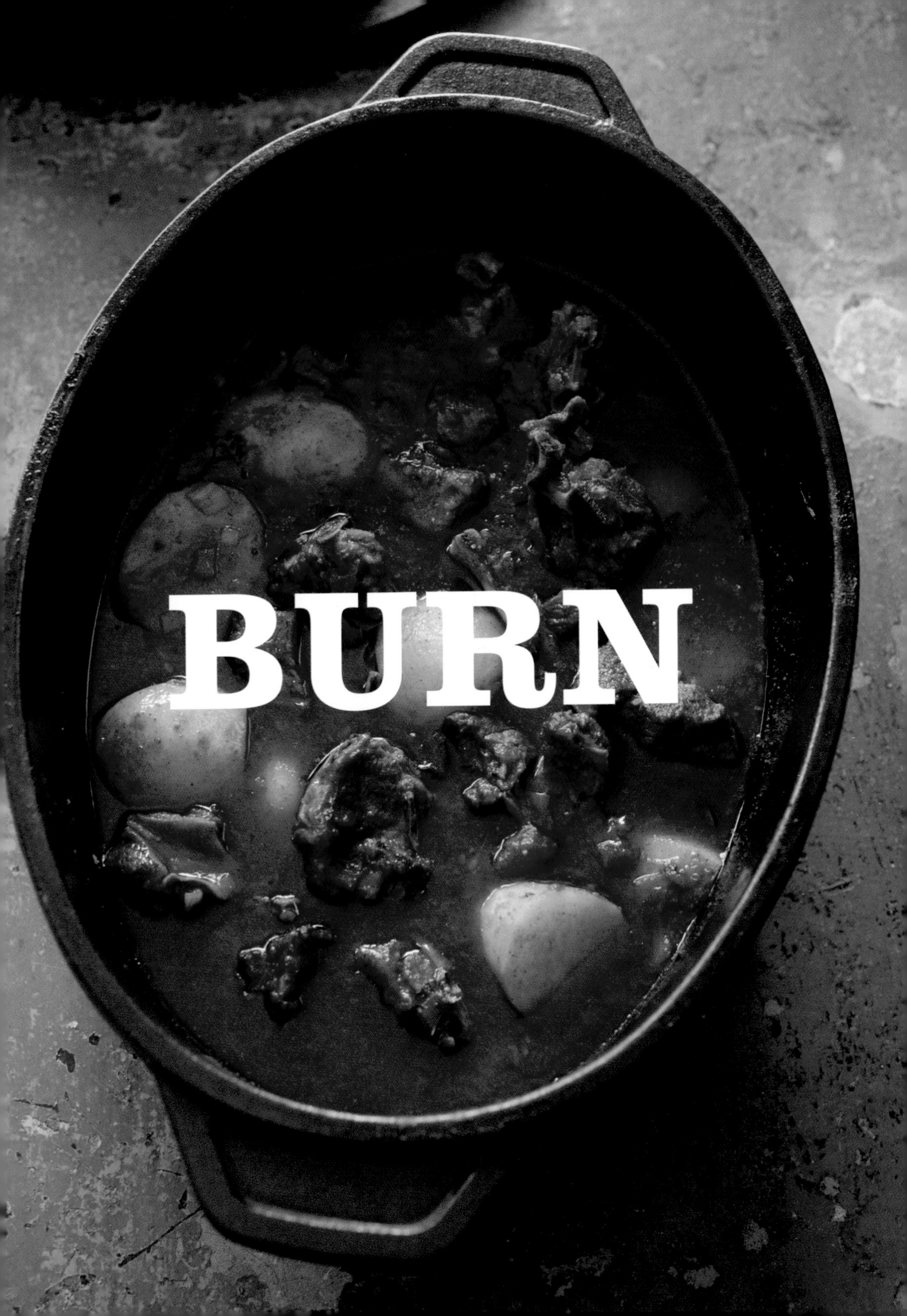

Aitchbone

1 aitchbone roast
30ml olive oil
3 large onions
1kg carrots
5 cloves of garlic
6 bay leaves
1 bottle dry red wine

Depending on how many guests you have to feed, you need a roast of between 1.3 and 1.8kg. The rule of thumb for meat is that you require 200g of meat per person with a little to spare, so we are talking about 6 to 8 guests here.

Preheat the oven to 140°C. You need a big pot, with a lid, that can go into the oven. Heat the olive oil in it on the stove top and brown the beef well on all sides. The oil should be spitting hot to seal the roast nicely. When you are done, leave the meat in the pot and add the roughly chopped onions and carrots, the whole garlic cloves, bay leaves and the bottle of wine. You can skimp and use cheap, box wine, but the results are better with a decent bottle.

Lift up the roast and let some of the vegetables form a little bed for it to sit on. Cover with the lid and place on a rack in the centre of the oven to cook slowly for 4 to 5 hours. Serve with crusty bread and green beans, or with mash and peas.

"The great thing about slow cooking is not only the flavour and tenderness of the dish, it's the ease of it."

Lamb Curry

1kg stewing lamb on the bone
50ml sunflower oil
10ml cumin seeds
5ml fennel seeds
10ml coriander seeds
10ml black mustard seeds
2 cardamom pods
5 whole cloves
1 cinnamon stick
2 chopped onions
10ml crushed garlic
10ml grated ginger
40ml fresh masala or curry powder
5ml turmeric powder
1 handful fresh curry leaves
400g tin chopped peeled tomatoes
250ml water
30ml apricot jam or chutney
salt

Brown the meat in oil and set aside. In a pan over a medium heat, dry-roast the cumin, fennel, coriander and mustard seeds together with the cardamom, cloves and cinnamon. When they start to brown slightly, remove from the heat and transfer to a spice grinder or mortar and pestle and grind to a powder.

Peel and quarter the potatoes. Halve and slice the onions, and fry in a little oil along with the garlic and ginger until they have softened. Add the masala, turmeric, ground spice mix and curry leaves, and stir well.

Return the meat to the pot and add the tinned tomatoes along with the water, chutney and potatoes. Season to taste, cover with a lid, and cook in a slow oven at about 140°C for 2 to 3 hours. Serve with rice or roti and some sambals.

"This is a very easy way to make a completely heroic curry."

Lentil & Sausage

500g brown lentils
6 to 8 rustic Italian sausages
5 peeled cloves of garlic
3 whole cloves
4 bay leaves
5ml smoked paprika
1 bottle dry white wine
750ml water
salt and pepper

Place the lentils in a bowl, cover with water and soak for at least an hour before you need them. Preheat your oven to 140°C.

Drain the lentils and place them in a cast-iron pot or heavy casserole dish with a lid. Add all the other ingredients to the container and give it a stir to mix everything in nicely. Cover with the lid and place on a rack in the centre of the oven to cook slowly for 5 to 6 hours.

Although the heat is very low and the lid seals it, you should check on it from time to time, adding a little water if necessary. This is a very hearty winter meal with bread and red wine, and it is excellent heated up as leftovers.

"Winter brings out my appetite for hearty, slow-cooked things like this casserole. It's best started in the morning for a late, lazy lunch."

Sausage & Beans

6 raw bratwurst
300g sugar beans
250ml dry white wine
100ml olive oil
1 carrot
1 onion
400g tin chopped tomatoes
500ml chicken stock
250g baby spinach leaves

If your butcher makes his own sausage, ask him for some advice, otherwise look for bratwurst at a German deli. If you twist each one in the middle, you can form 12 fat little sausages to go into the casserole.

Place the sugar beans in a bowl and cover them with cold water. Leave them to soak overnight. Preheat your oven to 140°C. Drain the beans and place them in a casserole dish with the wine and olive oil.

Grate the carrot and finely chop the onion and add this to the dish. Add the tin of tomatoes and the stock, arrange the sausages on top and cover with the lid. Place on a rack in the centre of the oven to cook for 2 hours before mixing in the ingredients and cooking for a further 30 minutes.

Ten minutes before the casserole is ready, wash and drain the spinach and fry it in batches in a pan with a little olive oil. Serve the casserole with rice and the flash-fried spinach.

"It's another casserole with sausages in it, I know, but the ease and the flavour make it impossible to leave it out of this book."

Sugar Beans

350g sugar beans
1 onion
1 large plum tomato
2 cloves garlic
1 bay leaf
2 sprigs parsley
1 sprig thyme
125ml white wine
250ml vegetable stock

Place the sugar beans in a bowl and cover them with cold water. Leave them to soak overnight. Preheat your oven to 120°C. Roughly chop the onion into big chunks and leave the tomato whole.

Drain the beans and place them in a casserole dish with a lid. Scatter the onion pieces over the beans and add the tomato, garlic cloves, bay leaf, parsley and thyme. Pour in the wine and the stock, put the lid on and place on a rack in the centre of the oven to cook for 3 to 4 hours, or until the beans are soft. Serve with crusty bread.

"OK, more beans, but they are good for you and they stretch the budget."

Chicken Casserole

1.5kg chicken leg-and-thigh pieces
3 lemons
1 onion, sliced
10ml crushed garlic
1 bunch sage
250ml dry white wine
olive oil

These days, it's quite hard to find chicken thighs with the leg attached. They are usually separated, but if you ask the butcher, he will sell you the attached portions. If you really battle to find them, regular thigh and leg portions will do. Don't use breasts though, as they are too dry for this dish.

Preheat the oven to 140°C. Heat a large ovenproof pot or a cast-iron pot on a medium to high heat and brown the chicken pieces in the olive oil. Remove them from the dish and set aside. Gently fry the onions and garlic in the same dish until they soften, and pour in the white wine. As it starts to bubble, scrape away any bits that have stuck to the base of the pot with a wooden spoon.

Halve the lemons and add them to the dish along with the browned chicken. Scatter the sage leaves over the whole dsih, cover with the lid and cook for 2 to 3 hours until the chicken is tender and almost falling off the bone. Serve with rice or mash and some greens.

"This is one of my staple winter dishes. It's tasty, wholesome and cheap to make."

My Steak Pie

500g rump or sirloin
30ml flour
salt and pepper
30ml olive oil
2 medium onions
500ml beef stock
60ml butter
60ml flour
250g brown mushrooms
1 roll frozen puff pastry
1 egg

Preheat your oven to 150°C. Cut the beef into 2.5cm cubes. Place the flour in a bowl and season with salt and pepper. Coat the meat in the flour and brown the pieces in the olive oil in a very hot pan. Transfer to an ovenproof dish.

Chop the onions and add them to the oil in the pan you've just used. Sauté until translucent, then add them to the meat along with the beef stock. Cook, covered, in the oven until the beef is soft, about 1 to 1½ hours.

Strain the liquid from the meat into a bowl and set the meat aside. Now melt the butter in a saucepan and whisk in the flour to form a paste. Remove from the heat and slowly pour in the reserved liquid, whisking constantly to avoid lumps forming. Return to the heat on a medium plate, whisking until the sauce thickens and comes to the boil.

Fry the sliced mushrooms in a little butter and add the beef and onion and the sauce to heat through. Spoon into individual serving dishes, then preheat your oven to 200°C.

Roll out the puff pastry on a floured surface and use a very sharp knife to cut lids to fit over the pie dishes. Brush with beaten egg and bake for 15 to 20 minutes, then reduce the temperature to 180°C and bake for a further 10 to 12 minutes, depending on the size of the pie.

"Once you try this, no more shop pies for you, guaranteed."

Calamari Stew

500g calamari tentacles and heads
500g calamari tubes
500g tomatoes
15ml sunflower oil
1 large onion
2 cloves garlic
250ml white wine
salt and pepper
1 sprig parlsey
1 bay leaf
1 sprig thyme

Preheat your oven to 150°C. Check that the tentacles and heads have been properly cleaned and slice the tubes into rings. Place the tomatoes in a bowl and stab them a few times with a sharp knife. Pour boiling water over them and leave them for 5 minutes, then drain and peel them.

Heat the oil in an ovenproof pot with a lid. Slice and gently fry the onion in the oil until it softens, then add the garlic, all the calamari, the wine, chopped tomato and salt and pepper. Make a bouquet garni by tying the parsley, bay leaf and thyme together with a piece of string and pop that in too. Close the pot with the lid and place in the oven to cook for 2 hours.

Check to see that the calamari is tender. It may need 100ml of water, a stir and another 30 minutes in the oven. Serve with buttery boiled potatoes.

"Most people really battle with calamari, getting it all rubbery when they cook it. This is wonderfully tender."

DESSERT

STORM

Chocolate Cups

200g dark chocolate (70%)
200g butter
4 eggs
4 egg yolks
120g sugar
75ml flour
250ml whipped fresh cream

Preheat your oven to 220°C, and lightly butter 6 tea cups, then place them in a baking dish. Pour some water into the baking dish so there's about 2cm of water in it.

Fill a saucepan to about one-third with water and set it on the stove to boil. Set a Pyrex or heat-proof glass bowl on top of the saucepan, like an inverted lid. The bottom of the bowl should not touch the water. Break up the chocolate and place it in the bowl with the butter, and allow them to melt together, stirring from time to time so the chocolate doesn't burn. Remove from the heat and set aside.

In a large bowl, beat together the eggs, egg yolks and sugar with an electric beater until light and fluffy. Add the chocolate mixture and the flour, then beat all the ingredients together quickly until smooth.

Divide the mixture evenly between the cups and carefully place the baking tray on a rack in the centre of the oven. Bake for 10 min. Serve each cup on a saucer with a teaspoon and whipped cream. Delicious when served either piping hot from the oven or at room temperature.

"This is just a crazy, chocolate buzz of a dessert. Everyone will request it again and again."

Tart in a Pan

10 ripe plums
60ml butter
125ml sugar
1 roll frozen puff pastry
icing sugar for dusting

Preheat your oven to 220°C. For this recipe you need a 25cm frying pan that is ovenproof. In other words, it shouldn't have a plastic handle.

Halve the plums and remove the pips. In the frying pan, over a medium heat, melt the butter and add the sugar: this will bubble and start to caramelise. Arrange the plums flesh-side down to fit tightly and fill the bottom of the pan. Work quickly and be careful not to burn yourself. Remove from the stove and set aside.

On a floured surface, lightly roll out the puff pastry, keeping it relatively thick. Use a sharp knife to cut a 25cm circle of pastry and fit it on top of the plums in the pan. Place the pan on a rack in the centre of the oven to bake for 25 to 35 minutes until the pastry is well risen and golden brown.

Remove from the oven and allow to cool for 5 minutes before inverting onto a plate. Serve with custard or cream.

"This is a variation of the French dessert tarte tatin which is made with apples. I make it all the time, changing the fruit with the seasons."

Apple Crumble with Raspberries

4 to 5 large Granny Smith apples
125g fresh raspberries
30ml butter
30ml sugar
30ml raspberry jam

Crumble
90g butter
90g ground almonds
90g sugar
125g flour

Preheat your oven to 180°C. Peel, core and cut the apples into chunks and place them in a bowl of water until needed. Wash and drain the raspberries. Smear the bottom and sides of a 20cm baking tin or ovenproof dish with the 30ml butter, sprinkle with the 30ml sugar and dot with raspberry jam.

Make the crumble by placing all the ingredients together in a mixing bowl. Using your fingertips, rub everything together repeatedly until it is all mixed together and takes on a crumbly consistency. Drain the apples and place them in the dish, scattering raspberries as you do, to disperse them throughout the pudding.

Cover the top completely with the crumble and bake in the oven for 30 to 40 minutes until cooked and golden brown. Serve with custard and cream.

"This is the first dessert I ever made. It's never failed me; You can't go wrong with apples and berries."

Ice-cream Sauces

Caramel
150g Wilson caramel squares
45ml fresh cream

Fill a saucepan to about one-third with water and set it on the stove to boil. Set a Pyrex or heat-proof glass bowl on top of the saucepan, like an inverted lid, but the bottom of the bowl should not touch the water. You could use a proper double boiler, but the bowl on the saucepan trick works perfectly.

Melt the caramel squares and cream together in the bowl until the caramels have completely dissolved. You should be stirring or whisking constantly to stop the sauce catching. This takes about 5 minutes and that's it. Serve with ice-cream, pour it over apple crumble or eat it out of a jug with a spoon.

Rocky Road
100g hazelnuts
1 bag pink and white marshmallows
200g dark chocolate
250ml fresh cream

In a small pan, over medium heat, roast the hazelnuts, shaking them around so that they get an even colour and don't burn. This will take about 7 to 10 minutes. Roughly chop the nuts into pieces and set aside. Use some scissors to snip the marshmallows into quarters and set aside.

Melt the chocolate and cream in a double boiler on medium heat and stir until the sauce is smooth. Stir in the nuts and marshmallows, and set aside to cool. (If the chocolate sauce is too hot, the mallows will melt.)

"Don't waste these recipes, only serve them with the best ice-cream. They are ridiculously good."

Sticky Toffee

375ml chopped pitted dates
375ml water
5ml bicarbonate of soda
125g butter
250ml sugar
3 eggs
500ml flour
3ml baking powder
2ml salt

Sauce
125g butter
30ml water
30ml golden syrup
250ml sugar
125ml fresh cream
125ml whisky

Preheat your oven to 180°C and lightly butter a large ovenproof baking dish. Place the dates and water in a small saucepan and bring to the boil, reduce the heat and allow to simmer for 5 minutes. Remove from the stove, stir in the bicarb and set aside.

Whisk the butter and sugar together until the mixture goes pale and creamy. Add the eggs one at a time, beating until well blended. Tip in the flour, baking powder and salt, blend these well and add the dates in their water, blending everything until smooth. Pour the mixture into the baking dish and bake in the centre of the oven for 35 to 45 minutes until the cake is firm to the touch.

Make the sauce by placing all the ingredients, except the whisky, in a saucepan. Bring to the boil over a medium heat, then reduce to simmer gently for 8 to 10 minutes. The sauce should thicken and become a deep golden colour. Stir in the whisky and remove from the heat.

Pour half the sauce over the pudding as soon as it comes out of the oven. Serve with cream or ice-cream and the rest of the sauce on the side.

"Cake and toffee. It's a no-brainer."

RIDING

SHOTGUN

Cucumber Pickle

To fill three to four 500ml glass jars

For the Brine
8 bay leaves
5ml whole black peppercorns
250ml white wine vinegar
500ml water
5ml salt
50ml sugar

4 English cucumbers
2 heads garlic

Place all the brine ingredients in a large pot and bring to the boil, stirring occasionally to ensure that all the sugar has dissolved. Remove from the heat and cool to room temperature.

Sterilise the jars and lids by washing them in hot soapy water and rinsing them thoroughly. Drain them on a dish rack. Preheat your oven to 100°C and place the jars in the oven for 10 minutes.

Slice the cucumbers into 1cm rounds. Peel and roughly chop all the garlic cloves. Fill the jars with cucumber slices and garlic, packing them as tightly as possible.

Pour the brine into the jars, filling them to the top. Pop 2 bay leaves in each bottle, seal with a lid and place in the fridge for at least a week before use. Once you have opened them, they will keep for up to 14 days in the fridge.

"These are meant for the hamburgers, but try them with cheese and brown bread."

Pickled Peppers

To fill four 500ml glass jars

For the Brine
1 red chilli
8 bay leaves
5ml whole black peppercorns
250ml white wine vinegar
500ml water
5ml salt
50ml sugar

6 large red peppers
6 large yellow peppers
2 large green peppers
1 head garlic

Sterilise the jars following the directions in the previous recipe for pickled cucumbers. Seed the peppers and cut the flesh into chunks. Fill the jars with pepper chunks and garlic, packing them as tightly as possible.

Seed and finely chop the chilli. Place it with the other brine ingredients in a large pot and bring to the boil, stirring occasionally to ensure that all the sugar has dissolved. Remove from the heat and pour immediately into the jars, filling them to the top. Pop 2 bay leaves in each bottle, and seal with a lid while hot.

Cool to room temperature before placing in the fridge. Allow at least a week before use to let the flavours develop. Once you have opened them, they will keep for up to 14 days in the fridge.

"These add zing to the sosaties, but can be added to pickles and cheese with bread."

Potato Salad

6 large potatoes
125ml olive oil
60ml white wine vinegar
5ml sugar
5ml Dijon mustard
salt and pepper

Leave the skins on the potatoes and place them in a large saucepan. Cover with water and set on the stove to boil. It should take about 30 minutes to cook them, but you can check by prodding one with a sharp knife. If it slides into the centre smoothly, the potatoes are done.

Remove from the heat, peel the potatoes with your fingers and cube them. Place the cubes in a bowl. Mix all the dressing ingredients together and stir until the sugar dissolves. Pour over the potatoes while they are still hot and cool to room temperature before serving.

Mashed Potato

6 large potatoes
100g butter
125 to 150ml milk
salt and pepper

Peel and halve the potatoes and place them in a large saucepan. Cover with water and add the 10ml of salt. Bring to the boil, then reduce the heat to medium and simmer for 30 minutes, or until soft. You can do the knife test again, as above. Remove from the heat and drain in a colander.

Return the potatoes to the cooking pot, add the butter and season. Start breaking them up with a masher, adding a little milk as you go. Keep adding milk and mashing until your desired consistency is reached. Different potatoes will absorb varying amounts of liquid. Serve hot.

Oven Chips

1kg small, waxy or red-skinned potatoes
30ml olive oil
15ml brown bread flour
salt and pepper

Preheat your oven to 220°C. Drizzle the oil to coat the base of a roasting tin and place it in the oven to get sizzling hot. Slice the potatoes into wedges, leaving the skin on, and add to the hot oil, tossing to coat well.

Bake for 20 minutes, then turn the potatoes and lightly sprinkle with the flour and bake for another 20 minutes or until the potatoes are golden brown and cooked through.

Regular Rice

250ml rice
525ml water
5ml salt

Pour the rice into a saucepan, add the water, cover with a lid and place on the stove over a high heat. Bring to the boil and turn the heat down to medium to allow a vigorous simmer for 15 minutes.

Remove from the stove and run cold water into the pot until it is no longer cloudy. Drain the water until the water is 1cm above the rice. Add the salt and put the lid back on the pot. Return it to the stove on a high heat, and as soon as the water starts to boil, switch the stove off.

Leave the pot on the plate and allow the rice to steam until all the liquid is absorbed. This will take 30 minutes.

Salad Dressing

125ml extra virgin olive oil
60ml white wine vinegar
5ml sugar
salt and pepper

This is a basic dressing that will serve for any green salad you care to think of. Place all the ingredients into a measuring jug or a cup. Stir until the sugar dissolves and drizzle over the salad. You can make bigger batches and keep the dressing in a bottle in the fridge for up to 14 days.

Variations: You can replace the white wine vinegar with the same quantity of raspberry vinegar or lemon juice. You can also add 5ml Dijon or whole grain mustard, 5ml dried oregano, or 5ml chopped parsley or marjoram.

Green Salad

1 head cos or butter lettuce
½ English cucumber
12 baby tomatoes

The basic green salad is almost too simple to write a recipe for. Choose the freshest ingredients possible, shred the lettuce, slice the cucumber and halve the tomatoes, then put them all in a bowl and drizzle with dressing. You can add variations endlessly.

Variations: Try adding chunked avocado, finely sliced radish, sliced red onion, spring onions, feta cheese, green or black olives, croutons, steamed green beans or long-stem broccoli. How about sliced boiled egg? The list is as varied as the produce in your fridge.

My Greek Salad

1 head cos lettuce
1 English cucumber
1 avocado
5 plum tomatoes
100g feta cheese
100g olives

Separate the leaves of the lettuce, then cut the cucumber, avocado and tomatoes into manageable chunks. Cube the feta cheese and drain the olives. Arrange all the ingredients on a platter without mixing them together.

The idea is that people can help themselves to more of what they like and less of what they don't. Although it is not traditional, I add the lettuce as a filler. You could also put things like red onion slices and radishes into the mix.

Coleslaw

1 green cabbage
125ml olive oil
60ml white wine vinegar
60ml mayonnaise
5ml sugar
salt and pepper

Shred cabbage with a sharp knife and place half of it in a large mixing bowl. Combine the remaining dressing ingredients in a measuring jug and stir until the sugar is all dissolved. Pour half the dressing over the cabbage in the bowl and toss well. Add the remaining shredded cabbage, pour in the rest of the dressing and toss again before serving.

Fried Onions

4 medium onions
30ml olive oil
5ml table salt

This recipe and the one that follows are really for cooking on the fire. You can do them on a normal stove with excellent results, but I always keep a cast-iron skillet with my charcoal grill so I can cook these sides to go with steak.

Halve, peel and slice the onions. Heat the olive oil in the pan and add the onions. Sprinkle with salt and leave them until they start to brown. Stir from time to time, letting them brown nicely, but not burn. Serve with steaks, burgers, anything really.

Fried Oysters

200g oyster mushrooms
100g butter

The earthy richness of mushroom is the perfect foil for steak. I particularly like the flavour of oyster mushrooms, and although they were hard to come by until very recently, you can find them in any supermarket now.

Slice the mushrooms into 1cm strips. Heat the butter in the pan until it looks like it is browning, then add the mushrooms. Move them around as they brown, but don't let them burn.

Griddled Leeks

1 punnet young leeks
30ml olive oil

Wash the leeks thoroughly, as they tend to have soil trapped in the outer layer. Heat the grill pan until it's smoking. Turn the heat down to medium, add the olive oil and simply grill the leeks, turning regularly until they soften.

You can griddle baby marrows, peppers and sliced aubergines in the same way and serve them with meat or in a robust salad.

Roast Butternut

2 medium butternuts
50ml butter
5ml ground cinnamon
1 lemon
15ml honey
salt and pepper

Preheat your oven to 200°C. Place the butternuts, whole, in a roasting pan. Roast them on a rack in the centre of the oven for 45 minuts until the skin is noticeably soft. Remove from the oven, halve and scoop out the pips.

In a saucepan over a medium heat, melt the butter and add the cinnamon, the juice of the lemon and the honey. Stir until the honey is all dissolved and season with salt and pepper. Pour this mixture over the butternuts and return to the oven for 20 minutes. Remove and serve.

Tomato Sauce

4kg ripe, red tomatoes
300ml white wine vinegar
200g castor sugar
8 cloves
5ml grated ginger
5ml grated nutmeg
3ml white peppercorns
3 bay leaves
5ml salt

Roughly chop the tomatoes and place in a large pot with all the other ingredients. Let it stand for 30 minutes to allow the flavours to combine and develop. Place on the stove over a medium heat and bring to the boil, simmer for 30 minutes until it starts to thicken and becomes aromatic.

Pass the sauce through a sieve to extract the peppercorns and bay leaves and any other chunks. Adjust the seasoning if necessary, then return to the pot and bring back to the boil and simmer until the sauce has reached the consistency of tomato sauce, which may take 60 to 90 minutes.

Transfer to sterilised bottles and seal them while the sauce is hot. Once they have cooled to room temperature, place the bottles in the fridge. You can use it immediately, but it is best to leave the sauce for a few days. Once you open a bottle, it will keep in the fridge for 14 days or so.

A note on sterilising bottles: The method outlined in the recipe for cucumber pickle (on page 138) is a surefire way to sterilise, but certain dishwashers also provide the function of sterilising jars. If you have one like this, the task is even easier.

"Be careful with this recipe. Your friends and family are going to bug you to make it for them."

Devilled Mustard

100g soft butter
30ml lemon juice
30ml Worcestershire sauce
15ml Dijon mustard
15ml wholegrain mustard
salt and pepper

Make a batch of this on the day you need it, though you can keep it to slather on anything you eat for the next 2 or 3 days. Soften the butter in a bowl and use a metal spoon to stir in all the other ingredients one by one. Use it on beef or chicken.

Mushroom Sauce

500g button mushrooms
30ml butter
30ml olive oil
5ml crushed garlic
250ml cream
30ml chopped parsley
salt and pepper

Thinly slice the mushrooms and heat the butter and olive oil in a large frying pan. Fry the mushrooms over a high heat to brown them for 5 minutes. Add the garlic and cream and season to taste. Reduce the heat and simmer until the sauce thickens, reducing the liquid by one-third. Stir in the parsley just before serving. Delicious with steaks or on toast with scrambled eggs, or rolled in pancakes with cheese.

"Although I expect that you will treasure
BLOKE as if it were the jersey of your
favourite player from the last World Cup,
I sincerely hope that it is not the last recipe
book you will ever own.

Food is not just about giving your body fuel
to burn, it is the glue of a healthy social life.
Getting some killer recipes under your belt
is just the beginning, and once you start to
explore the art, a whole new world awaits. It
might start in the pages of this book or you
may find an Italian or Asian title that gets you
started. Whatever. Just cook something and
see where it goes.

My love of cooking has allowed me to see the
world and meet some amazing people. I am
forever grateful to my mother who thought
it was nonsense that men didn't need to cook
and told me that if I wanted to hunt or fish I'd
have to cook the catch.

I am also grateful to everyone who has ever
enjoyed a meal I cooked, or shared a recipe
that has ended up in my repertoire."

a cookbook by Jason Comins